TO

FROM

DATE

We're all superheroes, you know. Maybe not exactly like what we see in the movies. But God says we're way more capable and amazing than we give Him credit for. We're more capable than we give Him credit for? Did I read that right, you ask? Yes, you did! Our abilities are directly related to our trust in God's power to do incredible things with, for, and through us. Maybe we won't be mistaken for a bird or an airplane anytime soon, but He says we can leap over walls (Psalm 18:29). With a mustard seed's worth of faith, we can tell mountains what to do (Matthew 17:20). And when we lean into Him, we can expect immeasurably more than all we can ask or imagine (Ephesians 3:20).

This journal is a place for you to discover, document, and delight in all you can do with God's might in you. It's a place to dream about possibilities and a place to plan them out. And it's a place where you can encourage yourself to stay amazing—because self-care can be part of loving yourself and preparing for the big things God has for you! Make each day your own by reading, reflecting, and writing your own thoughts. Then take it to the streets by sharing your inner strength with the world around you.

You probably don't even know how much this world needs the superhero version of you. As you interact with this journal, we're praying that you and God accomplish more than you've ever imagined.

ALL THINGS ARE POSSIBLE

INTERACTIVE | INSPIRATIONAL JOURNAL

DaySpring
LIVE YOUR FAITH

SCRIPTURE

THANK YOU FOR MAKING ME
SO WONDERFULLY COMPLEX!
YOUR WORKMANSHIP IS MARVELOUS—
HOW WELL I KNOW IT.

PSALM 139:14 NLT

GRATITUDE

Thank God for three things that make the view outside your window today beautiful:

1.

2.

3.

WELLNESS

Sip or guzzle? Every drop counts. How much water did you get today?

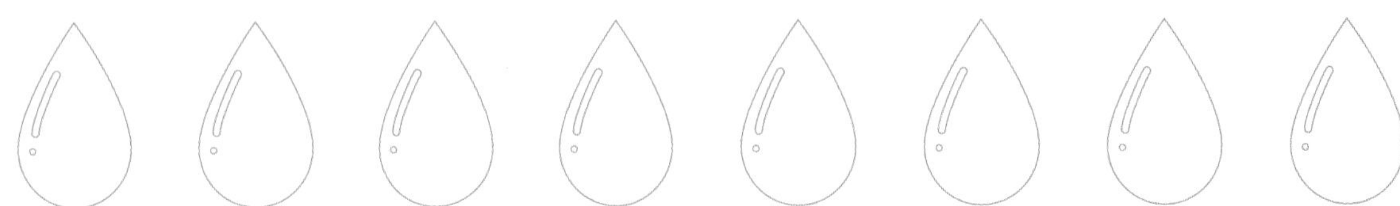

PRAYER

Lord, in light of being Your workmanship, my prayer is . . .

AMEN.

REFLECTION

As a marvelous workmanship of God, what are some ways you can uniquely shine today?

KINDNESS

Some of the best secrets are kept between you and God. Is there something encouraging you can do, say, or offer that no one else will know about? Write your ideas here, and then carry them out.

SCRIPTURE

IF ANYONE IS IN CHRIST,

THE NEW CREATION HAS COME:

THE OLD HAS GONE,

THE NEW IS HERE!

II CORINTHIANS 5:17 NIV

GRATITUDE

Thank God for something new.

WELLNESS

Fitness Goals

I am doing well with

I need to improve on

My strengths are

My weaknesses are

PRAYER

God, as a new creation in You, my prayer is . . .

AMEN.

REFLECTION

Like a butterfly whose DNA still looks like the caterpillar's, the creature itself has been totally reborn. You are a new creation. In what ways do you feel new?

KINDNESS

As you pray, does a friend or family member come to mind? God may be nudging you to reach out to them. Take a moment to text someone and remind them how important they are to you and God. Who did you text? What was their response?

SCRIPTURE

BE STRONG AND COURAGEOUS,

DO NOT BE AFRAID . . .

FOR THE LORD YOUR GOD IS THE ONE

WHO IS GOING WITH YOU.

HE WILL NOT DESERT YOU OR ABANDON YOU.

DEUTERONOMY 31:6 NASB

GRATITUDE

Thank God for someone brave.

WELLNESS

How many hours did you sleep last night? .... hours

PRAYER

Lord, knowing You are always with me, my prayer is . . .

AMEN.

REFLECTION

The very best vessels for His kingdom are those who say, "Okay, God, let's go after it! Use me however You want." What is an area you think God might be wanting you to grow?

KINDNESS

If you know God, then you know more about hope, love, and encouragement than most people! What kind words can you say to a stranger today? Write them down here and prepare for the moment to come.

SCRIPTURE

FOR THIS IS HOW GOD LOVED THE WORLD:
HE GAVE HIS ONE AND ONLY SON,
SO THAT EVERYONE WHO BELIEVES IN HIM
WILL NOT PERISH BUT HAVE ETERNAL LIFE.

JOHN 3:16 NLT

GRATITUDE

Thank God for something lost, then found.

WELLNESS

My stress management plan for the week is . . .

I can call (name a person who calms you)

I will (list activities you can do)

A positive statement I can say to myself is

PRAYER

God, in light of Your unfathomable love, my prayer is . . .

AMEN.

REFLECTION

Jesus is always the beginning of the journey, whether you've known Him forever or not at all. Who is Jesus to you?

KINDNESS

When you pray, you are sharing your compassion with others and your heart with God. Offer to pray for someone who is worried or hurting today. Write about your experience.

SCRIPTURE

I AM YOUR GOD.
I WILL STRENGTHEN YOU AND HELP YOU;
I WILL UPHOLD YOU WITH MY RIGHTEOUS RIGHT HAND.

ISAIAH 41:10 NIV

GRATITUDE

Thank God for something protected.

WELLNESS

How will you find rest today? (Check all that apply.)

- ☐ Take a nap. How long was the nap?
- ☐ Read a book. What was the title?
- ☐ Listen to music. Song or artist?
- ☐ Go to bed early. What time?
- ☐ Call a trusted friend. Who?
- ☐ Pray. What did you pray for?

PRAYER

"God, knowing Your strength and protection in my life, my prayer is . . .

AMEN."

REFLECTION

What are some ways you know God is taking care of you?

KINDNESS

Find a way to make someone's day. Write your experience here.

SCRIPTURE

THEY WHO SEEK THE LORD
WILL NOT LACK ANY GOOD THING.

PSALM 34:10 NASB

GRATITUDE

Thank God for a good thing in your life.

WELLNESS

Soothing face wash, cucumber eye pads, or night cream? How have you "hugged" your skin today?

PRAYER

Lord, knowing You promise to provide good things for me, my prayer is . . .

AMEN.

REFLECTION

Is there something you want? In the lines below, ask the Lord if it is good in His eyes. Then allow Him to lead you to the good things He's stored up for you today.

KINDNESS

Touch is one of the most vulnerable senses we have. Today, ask a trusted family member, coworker, or friend if they could use a hug. Then write about your experience here.

SCRIPTURE

GOD IS OUR REFUGE AND STRENGTH,
ALWAYS READY TO HELP IN TIMES OF TROUBLE.

PSALM 46:1 NLT

GRATITUDE

Thank God for trouble that brings Him close.

WELLNESS

What can you do today to help you feel healthy and strong?

- ☐ Read the Bible
- ☐ Go for a walk
- ☐ Drink more water
- ☐ Other (list below)
- ☐ Exercise
- ☐ Practice gratitude
- ☐ Encourage others
- ☐ Other (list below)

PRAYER

"God, as my refuge and strength, my prayer to You is . . .

AMEN."

REFLECTION

Even in the most desperate of times, God is always with us. How do you usually feel God's presence?

KINDNESS

Write about someone who made your life a little easier or better today.

SCRIPTURE

[LET US] NOT [GIVE] UP MEETING TOGETHER,
AS SOME ARE IN THE HABIT OF DOING,
BUT ENCOURAGING ONE ANOTHER—
AND ALL THE MORE AS YOU SEE THE DAY APPROACHING.

HEBREWS 10:25 NIV

GRATITUDE

Thank God for friends who encourage you.

WELLNESS

Sip or guzzle? Every drop counts. How much water did you get today?

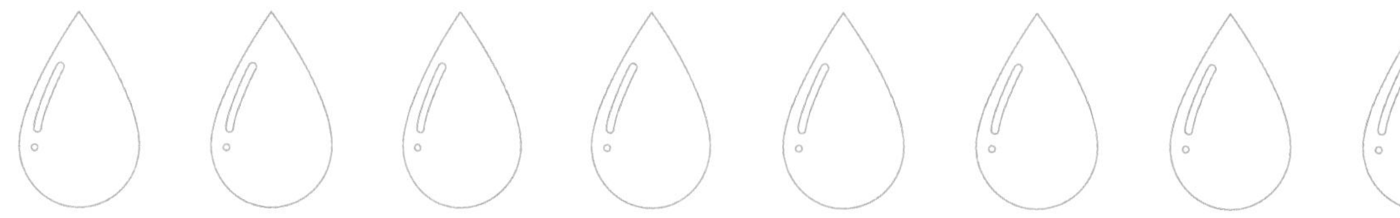

PRAYER

"Lord, with regard to gathering with others, my prayer is . . .

AMEN."

REFLECTION

Can you think of a time when you felt encouraged by others?

KINDNESS

Some of the best secrets are kept between you and God. Is there something encouraging you can do, say, or offer that no one else will know about? Write your ideas here, and then carry them out.

SCRIPTURE

EVERY GOOD THING GIVEN
AND EVERY PERFECT GIFT IS FROM ABOVE,
COMING DOWN FROM THE FATHER OF LIGHTS.

JAMES 1:17 NASB

GRATITUDE

Thank God for gifts He's given today.

WELLNESS

Fitness Goals

I am doing well with

I need to improve on

My strengths are

My weaknesses are

PRAYER

God, with regard to Your good gifts, my prayer today is . . .

AMEN.

REFLECTION

God thinks about us all the time. He chooses His gifts according to what He knows will bless our hearts. How has He blessed you recently?

KINDNESS

As you pray, does a friend or family member come to mind? God may be nudging you to reach out to them. Take a moment to text someone and remind them how important they are to you and God. Who did you text? What was their response?

SCRIPTURE

GOD IS
SHEER MERCY AND GRACE;
NOT EASILY ANGERED,
HE'S RICH IN LOVE.

PSALM 103:8 THE MESSAGE

GRATITUDE

Thank God for the last time you needed a little extra grace.

WELLNESS

How many hours did you sleep last night? ________ hours

PRAYER

"Lord, Your loving-kindness toward me . . .

AMEN."

REFLECTION

Do you have a favorite Bible verse? Why is it your favorite?
How has God's Word changed you?

KINDNESS

If you know God, then you know more about hope, love, and encouragement than most people! What kind words can you say to a stranger today? Write them down here and prepare for the moment to come.

SCRIPTURE

I TELL YOU THE TRUTH,
IF YOU HAD FAITH EVEN AS SMALL AS A MUSTARD SEED,
YOU COULD SAY TO THIS MOUNTAIN,
"MOVE FROM HERE TO THERE," AND IT WOULD MOVE.
NOTHING WOULD BE IMPOSSIBLE.

MATTHEW 17:20 NLT

GRATITUDE

Thank God for mountains He has moved.

WELLNESS

My stress management plan for the week is . . .

I can call (name a person who calms you)

I will (list activities you can do)

A positive statement I can say to myself is

PRAYER

Father, I want my faith to . . .

AMEN.

REFLECTION

When you can't, God still can. All it takes is faith, patience, and connection to His heart. What is something that seems impossible to you right now?

KINDNESS

When you pray, you are sharing your compassion with others and your heart with God. Offer to pray for someone who is worried or hurting today. Write about your experience.

SCRIPTURE

COME NEAR TO GOD AND
HE WILL COME NEAR TO YOU.

JAMES 4:8 NIV

GRATITUDE

Thank God for His nearness today.

WELLNESS

How will you find rest today? (Check all that apply.)

- ☐ Take a nap. How long was the nap?
- ☐ Read a book. What was the title?
- ☐ Listen to music. Song or artist?
- ☐ Go to bed early. What time?
- ☐ Call a trusted friend. Who?
- ☐ Pray. What did you pray for?

PRAYER

"Lord, in light of Your promise to draw near, here is how I'm coming to You today . . .

AMEN."

REFLECTION

God waits until we're ready. But when we move, He moves. Is there an area of life in which you're ready to take a step forward?

KINDNESS

Find a way to make someone's day. Write your experience here.

SCRIPTURE

WHAT GREAT NATION IS THERE
THAT HAS A GOD SO NEAR TO IT
AS IS THE LORD OUR GOD
WHENEVER WE CALL ON HIM?

DEUTERONOMY 4:7 NASB

GRATITUDE

Thank God for being near.

WELLNESS

Soothing face wash, cucumber eye pads, or night cream? How have you "hugged" your skin today?

PRAYER

"Father, if Your love is as close to me as You promise, then . . .

AMEN."

REFLECTION

Like an attentive dad, our Father is right there. All the time. Sending little reminders of His love. How do you sense His love today?

KINDNESS

Touch is one of the most vulnerable senses we have. Today, ask a trusted family member, coworker, or friend if they could use a hug. Then write about your experience here.

SCRIPTURE

I'VE TOLD YOU ALL THIS SO THAT TRUSTING ME,
YOU WILL BE UNSHAKABLE AND ASSURED,
DEEPLY AT PEACE. IN THIS GODLESS WORLD
YOU WILL CONTINUE TO EXPERIENCE DIFFICULTIES.
BUT TAKE HEART! I'VE CONQUERED THE WORLD.

JOHN 16:33 THE MESSAGE

GRATITUDE

Thank God for His peace in your current circumstances.

WELLNESS

What can you do today to help you feel healthy and strong?

- ☐ Read the Bible
- ☐ Go for a walk
- ☐ Drink more water
- ☐ Other (list below)
- ☐ Exercise
- ☐ Practice gratitude
- ☐ Encourage others
- ☐ Other (list below)

PRAYER

"God, Your peace . . .

AMEN."

REFLECTION

Nothing is too little for Him. Nothing is too big. Everything that pertains to you matters to Him. How does His love for you make a difference in your day?

KINDNESS

Write about someone who made your life a little easier or better today.

SCRIPTURE

GIVE ALL YOUR WORRIES
AND CARES TO GOD,
FOR HE CARES ABOUT YOU.

I PETER 5:7 NLT

GRATITUDE

Thank God that He wants to lift anxiety off your shoulders.

WELLNESS

Sip or guzzle? Every drop counts. How much water did you get today?

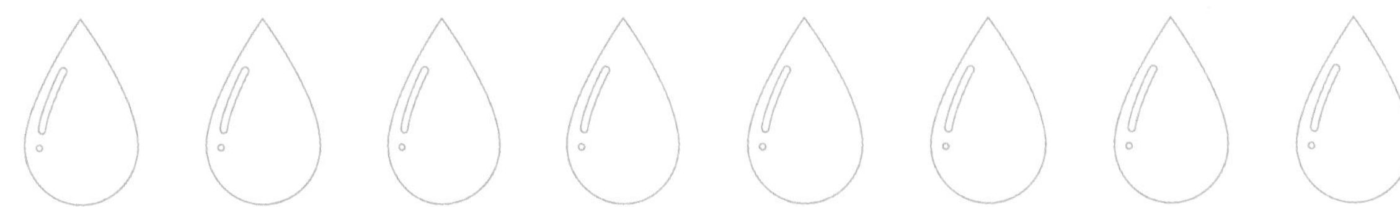

PRAYER

"Lord, I struggle with anxiety in these areas . . .

AMEN."

REFLECTION

Jesus doesn't want us to carry anything that could harm us or weigh us down, but He Himself can handle everything that concerns us! How does this affect your choices today?

KINDNESS

Some of the best secrets are kept between you and God. Is there something encouraging you can do, say, or offer that no one else will know about? Write your ideas here, and then carry them out.

SCRIPTURE

I AM WITH YOU ALWAYS,

TO THE END OF THE AGE.

MATTHEW 28:20 NASB

GRATITUDE

Thank God for always being there.

WELLNESS

Fitness Goals

I am doing well with

I need to improve on

My strengths are

My weaknesses are

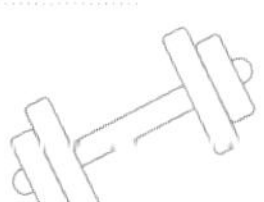

PRAYER

God, when I think of being with You forever . . .

AMEN.

REFLECTION

Jesus sent the Spirit of God as a gift. He offers comfort, guidance, wisdom, and a hope for the infinite treasures of heaven. How does the Holy Spirit work in your life?

KINDNESS

As you pray, does a friend or family member come to mind? God may be nudging you to reach out to them. Take a moment to text someone and remind them how important they are to you and God. Who did you text? What was their response?

SCRIPTURE

ASK ME AND I WILL TELL YOU
REMARKABLE SECRETS YOU DO NOT KNOW
ABOUT THINGS TO COME.

JEREMIAH 33:3 NLT

GRATITUDE

Thank God for having plans for your life.

WELLNESS

How many hours did you sleep last night? ______ hours

PRAYER

"Lord, sometimes I wonder . . .

AMEN."

REFLECTION

God's answers often come through experience because by knowing, instead of just hearing, we get all the feelings and understanding that can come no other way. How have you experienced God lately?

KINDNESS

If you know God, then you know more about hope, love, and encouragement than most people! What kind words can you say to a stranger today? Write them down here and prepare for the moment to come.

SCRIPTURE

SOME TRUST IN
CHARIOTS AND SOME IN HORSES,
BUT WE TRUST IN
THE NAME OF THE LORD OUR GOD.

PSALM 20:7 NIV

GRATITUDE

Thank God for His trustworthiness.

WELLNESS

My stress management plan for the week is . . .

I can call (name a person who calms you)

I will (list activities you can do)

A positive statement I can say to myself is

PRAYER

"Lord, I trust you with . . .

AMEN."

REFLECTION

People in their power are not even the tiniest fraction of God in His. What is something you know God can do better than you can?

KINDNESS

When you pray, you are sharing your compassion with others and your heart with God. Offer to pray for someone who is worried or hurting today. Write about your experience.

SCRIPTURE

"FOR I KNOW THE PLANS THAT I HAVE FOR YOU,"
DECLARES THE LORD,
"PLANS FOR PROSPERITY AND NOT FOR DISASTER,
TO GIVE YOU A FUTURE AND A HOPE."

JEREMIAH 29:11 NASB

GRATITUDE

Thank God for knowing more than you.

WELLNESS

How will you find rest today? (Check all that apply.)

- ☐ Take a nap. How long was the nap?
- ☐ Read a book. What was the title?
- ☐ Listen to music. Song or artist?
- ☐ Go to bed early. What time?
- ☐ Call a trusted friend. Who?
- ☐ Pray. What did you pray for?

PRAYER

"Father, regarding my future, my prayer is . . .

AMEN."

REFLECTION

We may not know exactly what's coming, but we can trust it's going to be good. How are you trusting God today?

KINDNESS

Find a way to make someone's day. Write your experience here.

SCRIPTURE

SO LET'S NOT ALLOW OURSELVES
TO GET FATIGUED DOING GOOD.
AT THE RIGHT TIME WE WILL HARVEST
A GOOD CROP IF WE DON'T GIVE UP, OR QUIT.

GALATIANS 6:9 THE MESSAGE

GRATITUDE

Thank God for keeping you strong.

WELLNESS

Soothing face wash, cucumber eye pads, or night cream? How have you "hugged" your skin today?

PRAYER

"God, I want to serve You. My prayer today is . . .

AMEN."

REFLECTION

Jesus can do so much through us, if we let Him. How do you enjoy serving others?

KINDNESS

Touch is one of the most vulnerable senses we have. Today, ask a trusted family member, coworker, or friend if they could use a hug. Then write about your experience here.

SCRIPTURE

WAIT PATIENTLY FOR THE LORD.

BE BRAVE AND COURAGEOUS.

YES, WAIT PATIENTLY FOR THE LORD.

PSALM 27:14 NLT

GRATITUDE

Thank God for giving you courage.

WELLNESS

What can you do today to help you feel healthy and strong?

- ☐ Read the Bible
- ☐ Exercise
- ☐ Go for a walk
- ☐ Practice gratitude
- ☐ Drink more water
- ☐ Encourage others
- ☐ Other (list below)
- ☐ Other (list below)

PRAYER

Father, it can be hard to wait. My prayer today is . . .

AMEN.

REFLECTION

God only asks us to do what we can. He will do what we can't. Does this change anything about how you'll view your day today?

KINDNESS

Write about someone who made your life a little easier or better today.

SCRIPTURE

IN THE MORNING, LORD,

YOU HEAR MY VOICE;

IN THE MORNING

I LAY MY REQUESTS BEFORE YOU

AND WAIT EXPECTANTLY.

PSALM 5:3 NIV

GRATITUDE

Thank God for listening to you.

WELLNESS

Sip or guzzle? Every drop counts. How much water did you get today?

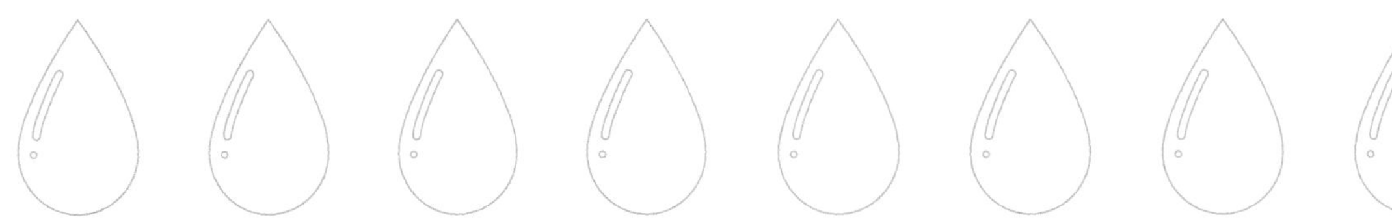

PRAYER

"Lord, with regard to my mornings, my prayer is . . .

AMEN."

REFLECTION

If you learn to place your expectation in God alone—believing that He is good and that He will do good—you will not be disappointed. Where are you placing your expectations today?

KINDNESS

Some of the best secrets are kept between you and God. Is there something encouraging you can do, say, or offer that no one else will know about? Write your ideas here, and then carry them out.

SCRIPTURE

THEREFORE, IF YOU HAVE BEEN RAISED WITH CHRIST,
KEEP SEEKING THE THINGS THAT ARE ABOVE,
WHERE CHRIST IS, SEATED AT THE RIGHT HAND OF GOD.

COLOSSIANS 3:1 NASB

GRATITUDE

Thank God for calling you to higher and bigger things.

WELLNESS

Fitness Goals

I am doing well with

I need to improve on

My strengths are

My weaknesses are

PRAYER

"God, with regard to keeping my mind on holy things . . .

AMEN."

REFLECTION

The Lord invites us to come see things from His point of view. All we need to do is ask. Consider some things you may want His perspective on today.

KINDNESS

As you pray, does a friend or family member come to mind? God may be nudging you to reach out to them. Take a moment to text someone and remind them how important they are to you and God. Who did you text? What was their response?

SCRIPTURE

WE ALSO PRAY THAT YOU WILL BE STRENGTHENED
WITH ALL HIS GLORIOUS POWER
SO YOU WILL HAVE ALL THE ENDURANCE
AND PATIENCE YOU NEED.
MAY YOU BE FILLED WITH JOY.

COLOSSIANS 1:11 NLT

GRATITUDE

Thank God for endurance.

WELLNESS

How many hours did you sleep last night? ______ hours

PRAYER

"Lord, when I think of being saved by You, my prayer is . . .

AMEN."

REFLECTION

God has handpicked each of us, given us everything we need, and empowered us to bring light wherever we go! How does knowing this influence your thinking?

KINDNESS

If you know God, then you know more about hope, love, and encouragement than most people! What kind words can you say to a stranger today? Write them down here and prepare for the moment to come.

SCRIPTURE

LET'S HOLD FIRMLY TO THE CONFESSION
OF OUR HOPE WITHOUT WAVERING,
FOR HE WHO PROMISED IS FAITHFUL.

HEBREWS 10:23 NASB

GRATITUDE

Thank God for the power of hope.

WELLNESS

My stress management plan for the week is . . .

I can call (name a person who calms you)

I will (list activities you can do)

A positive statement I can say to myself is

PRAYER

God, regarding Your faithfulness to me, my prayer is . . .

AMEN.

REFLECTION

Even if we haven't seen a particular miracle in our own lives before, we can be sure God can do it. Where in your life do you want to see a miracle happen?

KINDNESS

When you pray, you are sharing your compassion with others and your heart with God. Offer to pray for someone who is worried or hurting today. Write about your experience.

SCRIPTURE

HE COMFORTS US IN ALL OUR TROUBLES
SO THAT WE CAN COMFORT OTHERS.
WHEN THEY ARE TROUBLED,
WE WILL BE ABLE TO GIVE THEM
THE SAME COMFORT GOD HAS GIVEN US.

II CORINTHIANS 1:4 NLT

GRATITUDE

Thank God for His comfort in times of trouble.

WELLNESS

How will you find rest today? (Check all that apply.)

- ☐ Take a nap. How long was the nap?
- ☐ Read a book. What was the title?
- ☐ Listen to music. Song or artist?
- ☐ Go to bed early. What time?
- ☐ Call a trusted friend. Who?
- ☐ Pray. What did you pray for?

PRAYER

Father, regarding Your comfort when I need it, my prayer is . . .

AMEN.

REFLECTION

Our experiences serve to teach and train us about God and His character. Our experiences can also minister to others who go through similar pain. What hard times in your life has God used for others' good?

KINDNESS

Find a way to make someone's day. Write your experience here.

SCRIPTURE

CAST YOUR CARES ON THE LORD
AND HE WILL SUSTAIN YOU;
HE WILL NEVER LET
THE RIGHTEOUS BE SHAKEN.

PSALM 55:22 NIV

GRATITUDE

Thank God for a burden He has taken from you.

WELLNESS

Soothing face wash, cucumber eye pads, or night cream? How have you "hugged" your skin today?

PRAYER

"God, when I feel shaken, I pray . . .

AMEN."

REFLECTION

Casting cares on the Lord can mean giving Him whatever shreds you have and trusting Him to work them together for good (Romans 8:28). Do you have anything to hand over to Him today?

KINDNESS

Touch is one of the most vulnerable senses we have. Today, ask a trusted family member, coworker, or friend if they could use a hug. Then write about your experience here.

SCRIPTURE

THE LORD IS NEAR TO ALL WHO CALL ON HIM,
TO ALL WHO CALL ON HIM IN TRUTH.

PSALM 145:18 NASB

GRATITUDE

Thank God for a time you called on Him and He came.

WELLNESS

What can you do today to help you feel healthy and strong?

- ☐ Read the Bible
- ☐ Go for a walk
- ☐ Drink more water
- ☐ Other (list below)
- ☐ Exercise
- ☐ Practice gratitude
- ☐ Encourage others
- ☐ Other (list below)

PRAYER

"Lord, when I think of Your nearness, I pray . . .

AMEN."

REFLECTION

We've all needed the precise and life-saving help of the holy Healer. How has He touched you in healing?

KINDNESS

Write about someone who made your life a little easier or better today.

SCRIPTURE

I WILL GIVE YOU A NEW HEART,
AND I WILL PUT A NEW SPIRIT IN YOU.

EZEKIEL 36:26 NLT

GRATITUDE

Thank God for changing your heart and mind about something.

WELLNESS

Sip or guzzle? Every drop counts. How much water did you get today?

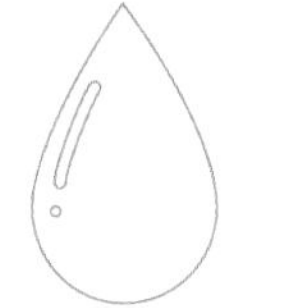
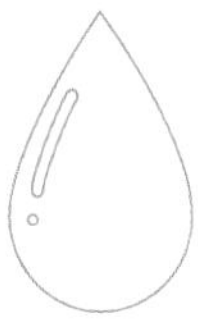
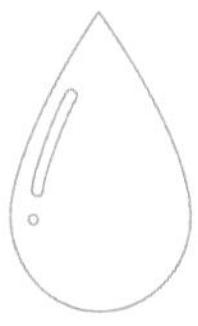
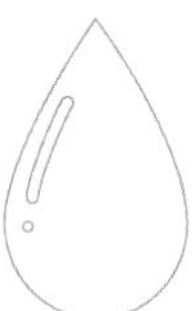
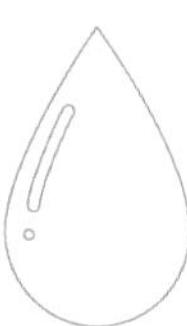

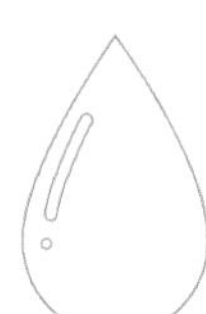

PRAYER

"God, You are the King of renewal. My prayer is . . .

AMEN."

REFLECTION

God doesn't need help, but He does want you to help. He's given you a role to play for His glory and your good. What is one way you enjoy serving Him and others?

KINDNESS

Some of the best secrets are kept between you and God. Is there something encouraging you can do, say, or offer that no one else will know about? Write your ideas here, and then carry them out.

SCRIPTURE

I CAN DO ALL THINGS
THROUGH HIM
WHO STRENGTHENS ME.

PHILIPPIANS 4:13 NASB

GRATITUDE

Thank God for accomplishing something amazing through you.

WELLNESS

Fitness Goals

I am doing well with

I need to improve on

My strengths are

My weaknesses are

PRAYER

"Lord, Your strength gives me strength to . . .

AMEN."

REFLECTION

When it's His plan and you're willing, you simply cannot fail.
What brave thing would you do right now if you knew you could with His help?

KINDNESS

As you pray, does a friend or family member come to mind? God may be nudging you to reach out to them. Take a moment to text someone and remind them how important they are to you and God. Who did you text? What was their response?

SCRIPTURE

YOU ARE FAMOUS, GOD,
FOR WELCOMING GOD-SEEKERS,
FOR DECKING US OUT IN DELIGHT.

PSALM 5:12 THE MESSAGE

GRATITUDE

Thank God for the favor He's shown you in a particular area.

WELLNESS

How many hours did you sleep last night? ________ hours

PRAYER

"God, when I think of Your favor surrounding me, my prayer is . . .

AMEN."

REFLECTION

What if your joy ran so deep that you just couldn't help brightening any room you entered?

KINDNESS

If you know God, then you know more about hope, love, and encouragement than most people! What kind words can you say to a stranger today? Write them down here and prepare for the moment to come.

SCRIPTURE

JESUS CHRIST IS THE SAME
YESTERDAY, TODAY, AND FOREVER.

HEBREWS 13:8 NLT

GRATITUDE

Thank God for being trustworthy.

WELLNESS

My stress management plan for the week is . . .

I can call (name a person who calms you)

I will (list activities you can do)

A positive statement I can say to myself is

PRAYER

"God, when I consider Your consistency and faithfulness, I pray . . .

AMEN."

REFLECTION

The only thing to be sure of is Jesus, the One who never changes. How can you lean on Him today?

KINDNESS

When you pray, you are sharing your compassion with others and your heart with God. Offer to pray for someone who is worried or hurting today. Write about your experience.

SCRIPTURE

THE EYES OF THE LORD
SEARCH THE WHOLE EARTH IN ORDER
TO STRENGTHEN THOSE WHOSE HEARTS
ARE FULLY COMMITTED TO HIM.

II CHRONICLES 16:9 NLT

GRATITUDE

Thank God for recognizing your hard work and faithfulness in a certain area.

WELLNESS

How will you find rest today? (Check all that apply.)

- ☐ Take a nap. How long was the nap?
- ☐ Read a book. What was the title?
- ☐ Listen to music. Song or artist?
- ☐ Go to bed early. What time?
- ☐ Call a trusted friend. Who?
- ☐ Pray. What did you pray for?

PRAYER

"Lord, with regard to Your support of me, my prayer is . . .

AMEN."

REFLECTION

The Lord watches for His faithful players. He carries the refreshment we need and eagerly fills our cup when we need it. In what ways do you most need to be refreshed?

KINDNESS

Find a way to make someone's day. Write your experience here.

SCRIPTURE

THE LORD YOUR GOD IS WITH YOU,
THE MIGHTY WARRIOR WHO SAVES.
HE WILL TAKE GREAT DELIGHT IN YOU;
IN HIS LOVE HE WILL NO LONGER REBUKE YOU,
BUT WILL REJOICE OVER YOU WITH SINGING.

ZEPHANIAH 3:17 NIV

GRATITUDE

Thank God for loving you big.

WELLNESS

Soothing face wash, cucumber eye pads, or night cream? How have you "hugged" your skin today?

PRAYER

"Father, Your love and joy change my life in these ways . . .

AMEN."

REFLECTION

It's easy to think of God as big and strong and powerful and holy, which He certainly is. But He also has a mother's touch for our gentle, childlike hearts. Who in your life needs God's gentle love today?

KINDNESS

Touch is one of the most vulnerable senses we have. Today, ask a trusted family member, coworker, or friend if they could use a hug. Then write about your experience here.

SCRIPTURE

THE LORD WILL ACCOMPLISH WHAT CONCERNS ME;
YOUR FAITHFULNESS, LORD, IS EVERLASTING;
DO NOT ABANDON THE WORKS OF YOUR HANDS.

PSALM 138:8 NASB

GRATITUDE

Thank God for keeping His promise in a certain way.

WELLNESS

What can you do today to help you feel healthy and strong?

- ☐ Read the Bible
- ☐ Go for a walk
- ☐ Drink more water
- ☐ Other (list below)
- ☐ Exercise
- ☐ Practice gratitude
- ☐ Encourage others
- ☐ Other (list below)

PRAYER

"God, I trust You to follow through with what You said . . .

AMEN."

REFLECTION

Asking questions isn't doubting God, if in asking you believe He has the answer. What is on your heart to ask Him today?

KINDNESS

Write about someone who made your life a little easier or better today.

SCRIPTURE

FIX YOUR ATTENTION ON GOD.

YOU'LL BE CHANGED FROM THE INSIDE OUT.

ROMANS 12:2 THE MESSAGE

GRATITUDE

Thank God for renewing your mind about a particular issue.

WELLNESS

Sip or guzzle? Every drop counts. How much water did you get today?

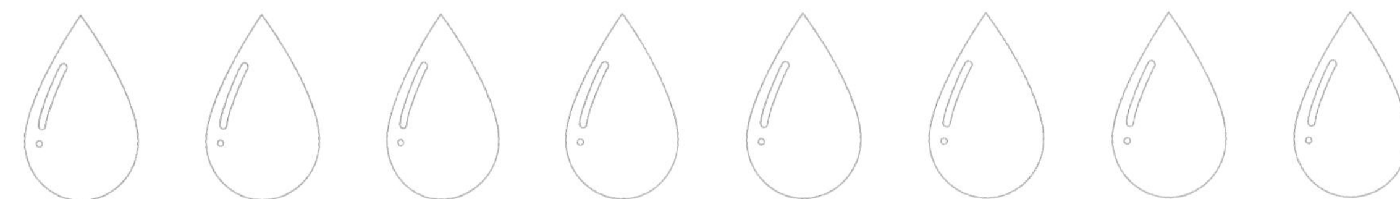

PRAYER

Lord, as You renew my mind, my prayer is . . .

AMEN.

REFLECTION

We can take the wheel and be responsible for all the road hazards and safe driving, or we can enjoy the scenery and go where God takes us. Do you tend to drive or sit back and enjoy the view?

KINDNESS

Some of the best secrets are kept between you and God. Is there something encouraging you can do, say, or offer that no one else will know about? Write your ideas here, and then carry them out.

SCRIPTURE

LOOK AT THE BIRDS.
THEY DON'T PLANT OR HARVEST OR STORE FOOD IN BARNS,
FOR YOUR HEAVENLY FATHER FEEDS THEM.
AND AREN'T YOU FAR MORE VALUABLE
TO HIM THAN THEY ARE?

MATTHEW 6:26 NLT

GRATITUDE

Thank God for a time He fulfilled your needs without you working hard at it.

WELLNESS

Fitness Goals

I am doing well with

I need to improve on

My strengths are

My weaknesses are

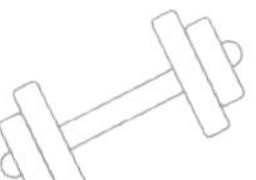

PRAYER

"Father, regarding my worth in Your eyes, my prayer is . . .

AMEN."

REFLECTION

God invites you to be raw and vulnerable before Him. In fact, that's when He does His best work. Is that generally hard or easy for you? Explain.

KINDNESS

As you pray, does a friend or family member come to mind? God may be nudging you to reach out to them. Take a moment to text someone and remind them how important they are to you and God. Who did you text? What was their response?

SCRIPTURE

HE CALLS HIS OWN SHEEP
BY NAME AND LEADS THEM OUT.

JOHN 10:3 NIV

GRATITUDE

Thank God for leading you in a certain way.

WELLNESS

How many hours did you sleep last night? .... hours

PRAYER

"Father, regarding hearing Your voice, my prayer is . . .

AMEN."

REFLECTION

The Bible says that the Spirit calls us and leads us. He never sends us on ahead to a place He hasn't been. How easy or hard is it for you to take big steps of faith?

KINDNESS

If you know God, then you know more about hope, love, and encouragement than most people! What kind words can you say to a stranger today? Write them down here and prepare for the moment to come.

SCRIPTURE

MY SHEEP LISTEN TO MY VOICE,

AND I KNOW THEM,

AND THEY FOLLOW ME.

JOHN 10:27 NASB

GRATITUDE

Thank God for showing you the way forward when you were struggling.

WELLNESS

My stress management plan for the week is . . .

I can call (name a person who calms you)

I will (list activities you can do)

A positive statement I can say to myself is

PRAYER

"God, as I listen for Your voice, my prayer is . . .

AMEN."

REFLECTION

God knew us even before we were in the womb (Jeremiah 1:5)! He has been speaking to us since the very beginning. What is one way you often "hear His voice" in your life? (If you're not sure, ask Him to show you.)

KINDNESS

When you pray, you are sharing your compassion with others and your heart with God. Offer to pray for someone who is worried or hurting today. Write about your experience.

SCRIPTURE

CONSIDER HIM WHO HAS ENDURED
SUCH HOSTILITY BY SINNERS AGAINST HIMSELF,
SO THAT YOU WILL NOT GROW WEARY AND LOSE HEART.

HEBREWS 12:3 NASB

GRATITUDE

Thank God for giving strength when you need it.

WELLNESS

How will you find rest today?

- ☐ Take a nap. How long was the nap?
- ☐ Read a book. What was the title?
- ☐ Listen to music. Song or artist?
- ☐ Go to bed early. What time?
- ☐ Call a trusted friend. Who?
- ☐ Pray. What did you pray for?

PRAYER

"Father, when I think of staying strong and not losing heart, my prayer is . . .

AMEN."

REFLECTION

Jesus knows brutal rejection—more than we will ever experience in our lifetime. But He also received the King's reward in the end. How does this knowledge affect you personally?

KINDNESS

Find a way to make someone's day. Write your experience here.

SCRIPTURE

SURELY YOUR GOODNESS AND LOVE
WILL FOLLOW ME ALL THE DAYS OF MY LIFE,
AND I WILL DWELL IN THE HOUSE
OF THE LORD FOREVER.

PSALM 23:6 NIV

GRATITUDE

Thank God for His persistent pursuit of you.

WELLNESS

Soothing face wash, cucumber eye pads, or night cream? How have you "hugged" your skin today?

PRAYER

Lord, with regard to Your goodness and mercy, my prayer is . . .

AMEN.

REFLECTION

You carry God's grace wherever you go, and you leave His grace with others when you share kindness and His love. How can you "leak" His goodness onto others?

KINDNESS

Touch is one of the most vulnerable senses we have. Today, ask a trusted family member, coworker, or friend if they could use a hug. Then write about your experience here.

SCRIPTURE

I HAVE LOVED YOU, MY PEOPLE,
WITH AN EVERLASTING LOVE.
WITH UNFAILING LOVE
I HAVE DRAWN YOU TO MYSELF.

JEREMIAH 31:3 NLT

GRATITUDE

Thank God for loving you through a difficult season.

WELLNESS

What can you do today to help you feel healthy and strong?

- ☐ Read the Bible
- ☐ Go for a walk
- ☐ Drink more water
- ☐ Other (list below)
- ☐ Exercise
- ☐ Practice gratitude
- ☐ Encourage others
- ☐ Other (list below)

PRAYER

"God, my prayer for Your love is . . .

AMEN."

REFLECTION

Remembering what God has done can build faith that He will do it again. Listening to others' stories can strengthen your own. Write down a testimony that changed your perspective.

KINDNESS

Write about someone who made your life a little easier or better today.

SCRIPTURE

EVEN THE VERY HAIRS
OF YOUR HEAD ARE ALL NUMBERED.

MATTHEW 10:30 NIV

GRATITUDE

Thank God for a time when you knew God was watching over you.

WELLNESS

Sip or guzzle? Every drop counts. How much water did you get today?

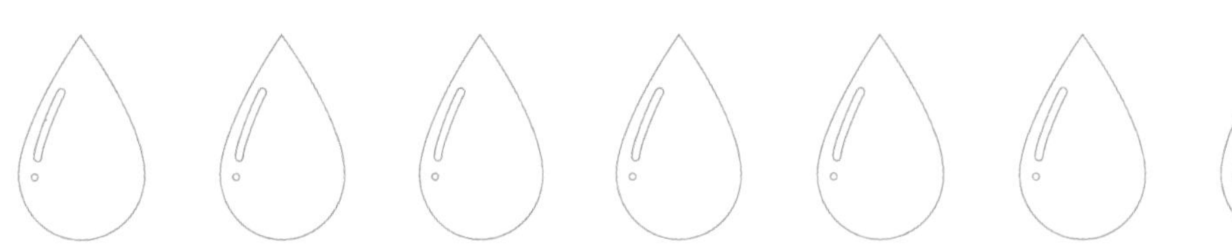

PRAYER

God, when I think about how well You know me, my prayer is . . .

AMEN.

REFLECTION

God is keenly aware of every single detail of every single life. He's the only one who really, truly gets you! How do you feel about that?

KINDNESS

Some of the best secrets are kept between you and God. Is there something encouraging you can do, say, or offer that no one else will know about? Write your ideas here, and then carry them out.

SCRIPTURE

YOU ARE TO CLING TO THE LORD YOUR GOD,

AS YOU HAVE DONE TO THIS DAY.

JOSHUA 23:8 NASB

GRATITUDE

Thank God for a time when you could rely on God when no one else was there.

WELLNESS

Fitness Goals

I am doing well with

I need to improve on

My strengths are

My weaknesses are

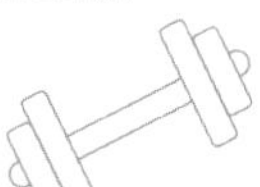

PRAYER

God, today I pray this as I cling to You . . .

AMEN.

REFLECTION

Sometimes it's easier to turn to the Lord when you're struggling but harder to remember when things are going great. How have you experienced this?

KINDNESS

As you pray, does a friend or family member come to mind? God may be nudging you to reach out to them. Take a moment to text someone and remind them how important they are to you and God. Who did you text? What was their response?

SCRIPTURE

TEACH US TO LIVE WELL!

TEACH US TO LIVE WISELY AND WELL!

PSALM 90:12 THE MESSAGE

GRATITUDE

Thank God for something beautiful about this day.

WELLNESS

How many hours did you sleep last night? ______ hours

PRAYER

"God, when I think of the days You've given me to live, my prayer is . . .

AMEN."

REFLECTION

You are desperately needed—your laughter, spunk, tenderness, compassion, and whatever gifts He has given you. Not a moment of your life is wasted in His book. Is that easy or hard for you to believe? Why?

KINDNESS

If you know God, then you know more about hope, love, and encouragement than most people! What kind words can you say to a stranger today? Write them down here and prepare for the moment to come.

SCRIPTURE

HAVE MERCY ON ME, O GOD,
BECAUSE OF YOUR UNFAILING LOVE.
BECAUSE OF YOUR GREAT COMPASSION,
BLOT OUT THE STAIN OF MY SINS.

PSALM 51:1 NLT

GRATITUDE

Thank God for His compassion for you.

WELLNESS

My stress management plan for the week is . . .

I can call (name a person who calms you)

I will (list activities you can do)

A positive statement I can say to myself is

PRAYER

Father, teach me to have greater compassion for . . .

AMEN.

REFLECTION

Nothing escapes the Lord's sight, and He will work all things for His glory. Just hang tight and watch Him do His thing. Is there something specific you're waiting on Him for?

KINDNESS

When you pray, you are sharing your compassion with others and your heart with God. Offer to pray for someone who is worried or hurting today. Write about your experience.

SCRIPTURE

HOW PRICELESS IS YOUR UNFAILING LOVE, O GOD!

PEOPLE TAKE REFUGE IN THE SHADOW OF YOUR WINGS.

PSALM 36:7 NIV

GRATITUDE

Thank God for a way He has been generous toward you.

WELLNESS

How will you find rest today? (Check all that apply.)

- ☐ Take a nap. How long was the nap?
- ☐ Read a book. What was the title?
- ☐ Listen to music. Song or artist?
- ☐ Go to bed early. What time?
- ☐ Call a trusted friend. Who?
- ☐ Pray. What did you pray for?

PRAYER

"Father, when I think of resting under Your wings, my prayer is . . .

AMEN."

REFLECTION

God's love is for everyone. Do you see little reminders of His love throughout your day? If so, what are they? If not, what could you add to your daily routine to remind you of His love?

KINDNESS

Find a way to make someone's day. Write your experience here.

SCRIPTURE

CALL UPON ME IN THE DAY OF TROUBLE;
I WILL RESCUE YOU, AND YOU WILL HONOR ME.

PSALM 50:15 NASB

GRATITUDE

Thank God for a time you were rescued from a dreary situation.

WELLNESS

Soothing face wash, cucumber eye pads, or night cream? How have you "hugged" your skin today?

PRAYER

"Lord, when I think of calling on You in trouble, my prayer is . . .

AMEN."

REFLECTION

God is not in the business of ignoring needs. The fact that you call on Him is a delight to His heart. Do you see Him as a place to run when you need something, or is that a challenging concept for you? Why?

KINDNESS

Touch is one of the most vulnerable senses we have. Today, ask a trusted family member, coworker, or friend if they could use a hug. Then write about your experience here.

SCRIPTURE

WORK WILLINGLY AT WHATEVER YOU DO, AS THOUGH YOU WERE WORKING FOR THE LORD RATHER THAN FOR PEOPLE.

COLOSSIANS 3:23 NLT

GRATITUDE

Thank God for your work.

WELLNESS

What can you do today to help you feel healthy and strong?

- ☐ Read the Bible
- ☐ Go for a walk
- ☐ Drink more water
- ☐ Other (list below)
- ☐ Exercise
- ☐ Practice gratitude
- ☐ Encourage others
- ☐ Other (list below)

PRAYER

"God, with regard to my work, my prayer is . . .

AMEN."

REFLECTION

What are some things you don't enjoy but that you could start thinking of as a way of serving God? Does that make them seem easier or harder?

KINDNESS

Write about someone who made your life a little easier or better today.

SCRIPTURE

BUT GODLINESS
WITH CONTENTMENT
IS GREAT GAIN.

I TIMOTHY 6:6 NIV

GRATITUDE

Thank God for the last time you felt truly content.

WELLNESS

Sip or guzzle? Every drop counts. How much water did you get today?

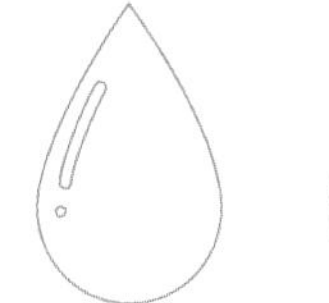 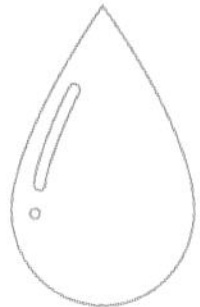 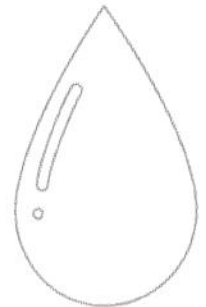 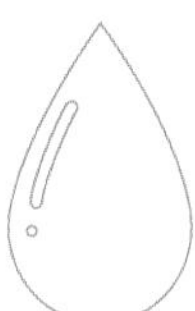 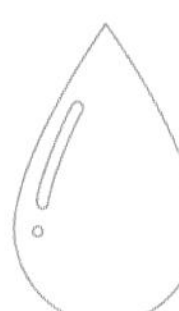 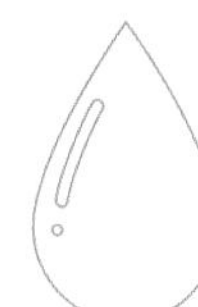 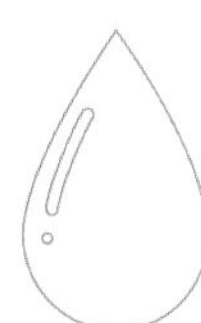 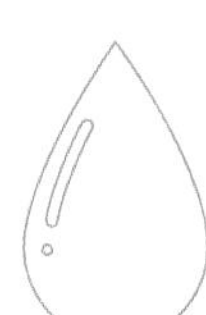

PRAYER

"Lord, help me to understand what godliness is in these areas . . .

AMEN."

REFLECTION

A life in God's hands leads to the most profound peace. When is the last time you sensed God's peace? Where were you? How did that feel?

KINDNESS

Some of the best secrets are kept between you and God. Is there something encouraging you can do, say, or offer that no one else will know about? Write your ideas here, and then carry them out.

SCRIPTURE

THE FEAR OF THE LORD

IS THE BEGINNING OF WISDOM.

PSALM 111:10 NASB

GRATITUDE

Thank God for His promise to give you wisdom.

WELLNESS

Fitness Goals

I am doing well with

I need to improve on

My strengths are

My weaknesses are

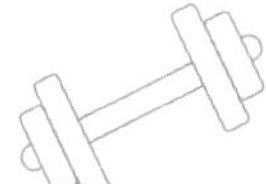

PRAYER

"Father, I ask for Your wisdom in these areas . . .

AMEN."

REFLECTION

Every experience you have can lead to the wisdom of God, if you ask for it and keep your eyes open. When was the last time you relied on God's wisdom to help you make a decision? How did things turn out?

KINDNESS

As you pray, does a friend or family member come to mind? God may be nudging you to reach out to them. Take a moment to text someone and remind them how important they are to you and God. Who did you text? What was their response?

SCRIPTURE

THIS IS THE VERY BEST WAY TO LOVE.

PUT YOUR LIFE ON THE LINE FOR YOUR FRIENDS.

JOHN 15:13 THE MESSAGE

GRATITUDE

Thank God for someone who has made sacrifices for you.

WELLNESS

How many hours did you sleep last night? ________ hours

PRAYER

"God, I lay my friendships down to You . . .

AMEN."

REFLECTION

God sees your true sacrifice and delights in it. Do you want to be noticed for your good work, or is it enough to know that God sees? Why?

KINDNESS

If you know God, then you know more about hope, love, and encouragement than most people! What kind words can you say to a stranger today? Write them down here and prepare for the moment to come.

SCRIPTURE

ONLY I CAN TELL YOU THE FUTURE
BEFORE IT EVEN HAPPENS.
EVERYTHING I PLAN WILL COME TO PASS,
FOR I DO WHATEVER I WISH.

ISAIAH 46:10 NLT

GRATITUDE

Thank God for the last good thing He gave you.

WELLNESS

My stress management plan for the week is . . .

I can call (name a person who calms you)

I will (list activities you can do)

A positive statement I can say to myself is

PRAYER

"God, I am trusting You in these ways today . . .

AMEN."

REFLECTION

The very definition of faith includes the requirement that you not be able to see into the future. Do you like to know what's coming, or do you like walking by faith? Why?

KINDNESS

When you pray, you are sharing your compassion with others and your heart with God. Offer to pray for someone who is worried or hurting today. Write about your experience.

SCRIPTURE

THEREFORE DO NOT WORRY ABOUT TOMORROW,
FOR TOMORROW WILL WORRY ABOUT ITSELF.
EACH DAY HAS ENOUGH TROUBLE OF ITS OWN.

MATTHEW 6:34 NIV

GRATITUDE

Thank God for a something you know He's working on for you.

WELLNESS

How will you find rest today? (Check all that apply.)

- ☐ Take a nap. How long was the nap?
- ☐ Read a book. What was the title?
- ☐ Listen to music. Song or artist?
- ☐ Go to bed early. What time?
- ☐ Call a trusted friend. Who?
- ☐ Pray. What did you pray for?

PRAYER

"Lord, I release these worries to You today . . .

AMEN."

REFLECTION

God isn't asking you to solve life. He only asks you to do the next thing. How do you navigate a healthy balance between worrying and letting things slide?

KINDNESS

Find a way to make someone's day. Write your experience here.

SCRIPTURE

FOR FROM DAYS OF OLD
THEY HAVE NOT HEARD OR PERCEIVED BY EAR,
NOR HAS THE EYE SEEN A GOD BESIDES YOU,
WHO ACTS ON BEHALF OF THE ONE WHO WAITS FOR HIM.

ISAIAH 64:4 NASB

GRATITUDE

Thank God for your five senses.

WELLNESS

Soothing face wash, cucumber eye pads, or night cream? How have you "hugged" your skin today?

PRAYER

Father, waiting on You can be difficult, but here is how I'm trying . . .

AMEN.

REFLECTION

People have searched for answers other than God, but they come up short every time. Do you consider Him your friend? If so, how do you describe your friendship with Him?

KINDNESS

Touch is one of the most vulnerable senses we have. Today, ask a trusted family member, coworker, or friend if they could use a hug. Then write about your experience here.

SCRIPTURE

THIS SAME GOD WHO TAKES CARE OF ME
WILL SUPPLY ALL YOUR NEEDS FROM HIS GLORIOUS RICHES,
WHICH HAVE BEEN GIVEN TO US IN CHRIST JESUS.

PHILIPPIANS 4:19 NLT

GRATITUDE

Thank God for the last thing you ate.

WELLNESS

What can you do today to help you feel healthy and strong?

- ☐ Read the Bible
- ☐ Go for a walk
- ☐ Drink more water
- ☐ Other (list below)
- ☐ Exercise
- ☐ Practice gratitude
- ☐ Encourage others
- ☐ Other (list below)

PRAYER

"Lord, as I trust You for my needs being met, my prayer is . . .

AMEN."

REFLECTION

What help do you need from our limitless God today?

KINDNESS

Write about someone who made your life a little easier or better today.

SCRIPTURE

WHEN I WAS DESPERATE,
I CALLED OUT,
AND GOD GOT ME OUT OF A TIGHT SPOT.

PSALM 34:6 THE MESSAGE

GRATITUDE

Thank God for an experience that turned out better than you expected.

WELLNESS

Sip or guzzle? Every drop counts. How much water did you get today?

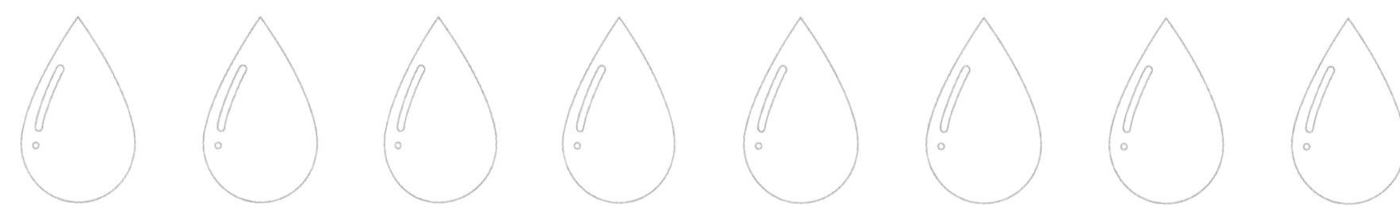

PRAYER

"God, when I think of how I cry out to You and how You respond, my prayer is . . .

AMEN."

REFLECTION

In the face of trouble, there is a wise One who leans in and whispers peace. Be still, and know that He is God. What makes you feel most peaceful?

KINDNESS

Some of the best secrets are kept between you and God. Is there something encouraging you can do, say, or offer that no one else will know about? Write your ideas here, and then carry them out.

SCRIPTURE

WHEN YOU PRAY, GO INTO YOUR ROOM,
CLOSE THE DOOR AND PRAY TO YOUR FATHER,
WHO IS UNSEEN. THEN YOUR FATHER,
WHO SEES WHAT IS DONE IN SECRET,
WILL REWARD YOU.

MATTHEW 6:6 NIV

GRATITUDE

Thank God for an answered prayer.

WELLNESS

Fitness Goals

I am doing well with

I need to improve on

My strengths are

My weaknesses are

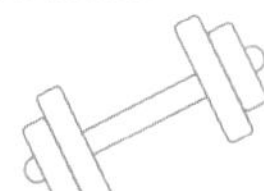

PRAYER

"Father, regarding my prayer life, I pray today that . . .

AMEN."

REFLECTION

Withdraw into the arms of God, and you will find a peace that passes understanding. What's your favorite way to take time to rest and pray?

KINDNESS

As you pray, does a friend or family member come to mind? God may be nudging you to reach out to them. Take a moment to text someone and remind them how important they are to you and God. Who did you text? What was their response?

SCRIPTURE

MY SOUL, WAIT IN SILENCE FOR GOD ALONE,

FOR MY HOPE IS FROM HIM.

HE ALONE IS MY ROCK AND MY SALVATION,

MY REFUGE; I WILL NOT BE SHAKEN.

PSALM 62:5-6 NASB

GRATITUDE

Thank God for the last time you truly felt God was your rock.

WELLNESS

How many hours did you sleep last night? ________ hours

PRAYER

"Father, as I wait for You, my prayer is . . .

AMEN."

REFLECTION

Sometimes it is hard to wait quietly for God. But He has a way of showing up at the perfect time when we do. What are you waiting on God for today?

KINDNESS

If you know God, then you know more about hope, love, and encouragement than most people! What kind words can you say to a stranger today? Write them down here and prepare for the moment to come.

SCRIPTURE

DON'T LET THE SUN GO DOWN
WHILE YOU ARE STILL ANGRY,
FOR ANGER GIVES A FOOTHOLD TO THE DEVIL.

EPHESIANS 4:26-27 NLT

GRATITUDE

Thank God for emotions—all of them!

WELLNESS

My stress management plan for the week is . . .

I can call (name a person who calms you)

I will (list activities you can do)

A positive statement I can say to myself is

PRAYER

"Father, with regard to how I handle anger, my prayer is . . .

AMEN."

REFLECTION

The very best thing to do when you've been offended is to forgive. Write down the name(s) of those who need to forgive, and then pray for each one of them.

KINDNESS

When you pray, you are sharing your compassion with others and your heart with God. Offer to pray for someone who is worried or hurting today. Write about your experience.

SCRIPTURE

I HAVE BEEN CRUCIFIED WITH CHRIST
AND I NO LONGER LIVE,
BUT CHRIST LIVES IN ME.

GALATIANS 2:20 NIV

GRATITUDE

Thank God for a new life in Christ.

WELLNESS

How will you find rest today? (Check all that apply.)

- ☐ Take a nap. How long was the nap?
- ☐ Read a book. What was the title?
- ☐ Listen to music. Song or artist?
- ☐ Go to bed early. What time?
- ☐ Call a trusted friend. Who?
- ☐ Pray. What did you pray for?

PRAYER

"Lord, when I think of Your willingness to make Your home in me, I pray . . .

AMEN."

REFLECTION

Because of Jesus, shame has no hold on you. Do you believe that you are free? How do you experience freedom?

KINDNESS

Find a way to make someone's day. Write your experience here.

SCRIPTURE

WHAT A GOD WE HAVE!
AND HOW FORTUNATE WE ARE TO HAVE HIM,
THIS FATHER OF OUR MASTER JESUS! . . .
WE'VE BEEN GIVEN A BRAND-NEW LIFE
AND HAVE EVERYTHING TO LIVE FOR.

I PETER 1:3 THE MESSAGE

GRATITUDE

Thank God for a time you got a second chance.

WELLNESS

Soothing face wash, cucumber eye pads, or night cream? How have you "hugged" your skin today?

PRAYER

"Father, my blessing for You today is . . .

AMEN."

REFLECTION

Mercy is receiving a reward that far outweighs what we deserve. Can you think of a time when you were shown incredible mercy?

KINDNESS

Touch is one of the most vulnerable senses we have. Today, ask a trusted family member, coworker, or friend if they could use a hug. Then write about your experience here.

SCRIPTURE

[GOD] USES US TO SPREAD
THE KNOWLEDGE OF CHRIST EVERYWHERE,
LIKE A SWEET PERFUME.

II CORINTHIANS 2:14 NLT

GRATITUDE

Thank God for the most beautiful thing you've seen today.

WELLNESS

What can you do today to help you feel healthy and strong?

- ☐ Read the Bible
- ☐ Go for a walk
- ☐ Drink more water
- ☐ Other (list below)
- ☐ Exercise
- ☐ Practice gratitude
- ☐ Encourage others
- ☐ Other (list below)

PRAYER

"Lord, I want to shine for You. My prayer is . . .

AMEN."

REFLECTION

What do you think it means to be the "sweet perfume" of Jesus everywhere we go?

KINDNESS

Write about someone who made your life a little easier or better today.

SCRIPTURE

WE DO NOT HAVE A HIGH PRIEST
WHO IS UNABLE TO EMPATHIZE WITH OUR WEAKNESSES,
BUT WE HAVE ONE WHO HAS BEEN TEMPTED IN EVERY WAY,
JUST AS WE ARE—YET HE DID NOT SIN.

HEBREWS 4:15 NIV

GRATITUDE

Thank God for a time He got you out of a tempting situation.

WELLNESS

Sip or guzzle? Every drop counts. How much water did you get today?

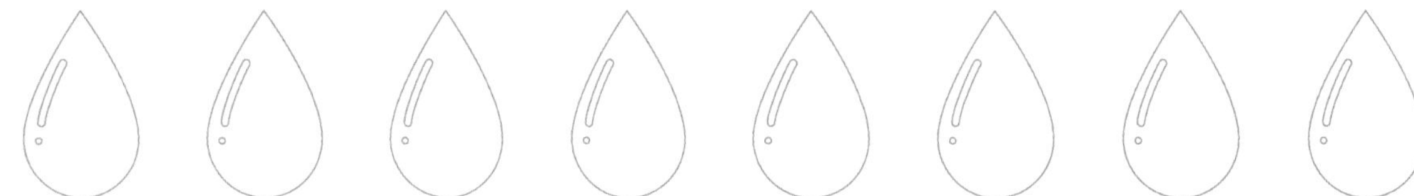

PRAYER

"God, when I think of the things that tempt me, my prayer is . . .

AMEN."

REFLECTION

How does knowing that Jesus was tempted but found strength through His Father affect your perspective on your own temptations and struggles?

KINDNESS

Some of the best secrets are kept between you and God. Is there something encouraging you can do, say, or offer that no one else will know about? Write your ideas here, and then carry them out.

SCRIPTURE

YOUR KINGDOM IS AN EVERLASTING KINGDOM,
AND YOUR DOMINION ENDURES
THROUGHOUT ALL GENERATIONS.

PSALM 145:13 NASB

GRATITUDE

Thank God for life beyond this one.

WELLNESS

Fitness Goals

I am doing well with

I need to improve on

My strengths are

My weaknesses are

PRAYER

"Father, You rule in every area of my life, including . . .

AMEN."

REFLECTION

God's love is what warms us from the inside out. His character of love is what allows us to feel loved and give love. How have you experienced His love today?

KINDNESS

As you pray, does a friend or family member come to mind? God may be nudging you to reach out to them. Take a moment to text someone and remind them how important they are to you and God. Who did you text? What was their response?

SCRIPTURE

YOU MUST LOVE THE LORD YOUR GOD
WITH ALL YOUR HEART, ALL YOUR SOUL,
AND ALL YOUR MIND.

MATTHEW 22:37 NLT

GRATITUDE

Thank God for something you're passionate about.

WELLNESS

How many hours did you sleep last night? ______ hours

PRAYER

"God, I give You all I have in these specific areas today . . .

AMEN."

REFLECTION

What do you think it might mean to love the Lord with all your mind?

KINDNESS

If you know God, then you know more about hope, love, and encouragement than most people! What kind words can you say to a stranger today? Write them down here and prepare for the moment to come.

SCRIPTURE

IF ANYONE LOVES ME,
HE WILL CAREFULLY KEEP MY WORD
AND MY FATHER WILL LOVE HIM—
WE'LL MOVE RIGHT INTO THE NEIGHBORHOOD!

JOHN 14:23 THE MESSAGE

GRATITUDE

Thank God for the Bible and your favorite Scripture.

WELLNESS

My stress management plan for the week is . . .

I can call (name a person who calms you)

I will (list activities you can do)

A positive statement I can say to myself is

PRAYER

"Father, as I seek to know and love You more, my prayer is . . .

AMEN."

REFLECTION

When we're brimming with hope and love, our kindness tends to overflow from our hearts into the world around us. How has your heart impacted those around you this week?

KINDNESS

When you pray, you are sharing your compassion with others and your heart with God. Offer to pray for someone who is worried or hurting today. Write about your experience.

SCRIPTURE

LOVE IS PATIENT, LOVE IS KIND.
IT DOES NOT ENVY, IT DOES NOT BOAST,
IT IS NOT PROUD. IT DOES NOT DISHONOR OTHERS,
IT IS NOT SELF-SEEKING, IT IS NOT EASILY ANGERED,
IT KEEPS NO RECORD OF WRONGS.

I CORINTHIANS 13:4–5 NIV

GRATITUDE

Thank God for someone who loves you unconditionally.

WELLNESS

How will you find rest today? (Check all that apply.)

- ☐ Take a nap. How long was the nap?
- ☐ Read a book. What was the title?
- ☐ Listen to music. Song or artist?
- ☐ Go to bed early. What time?
- ☐ Call a trusted friend. Who?
- ☐ Pray. What did you pray for?

PRAYER

"God, regarding living in love, my prayer is . . .

AMEN."

REFLECTION

God is love. Every characteristic that can be applied to love can be applied to God. Which of God's characteristics would you most like to see played out in your own life today?

KINDNESS

Find a way to make someone's day. Write your experience here.

SCRIPTURE

WE WALK BY FAITH,

NOT BY SIGHT.

II CORINTHIANS 5:7 NASB

GRATITUDE

Thank God for something you know for sure, even without tangible proof.

WELLNESS

Soothing face wash, cucumber eye pads, or night cream? How have you "hugged" your skin today?

PRAYER

"Lord, please build my faith in this area . . .

AMEN."

REFLECTION

It's great to know what's coming. But it's a gift to take steps forward, believing God and trusting in His promises. How are you walking by faith today?

KINDNESS

Touch is one of the most vulnerable senses we have. Today, ask a trusted family member, coworker, or friend if they could use a hug. Then write about your experience here.

SCRIPTURE

MAY HE GRANT YOUR HEART'S DESIRES
AND MAKE ALL YOUR PLANS SUCCEED.

PSALM 20:4 NLT

GRATITUDE

Thank God for the best thing that has ever happened to you.

WELLNESS

What can you do today to help you feel healthy and strong?

- ☐ Read the Bible
- ☐ Go for a walk
- ☐ Drink more water
- ☐ Other (list below)
- ☐ Exercise
- ☐ Practice gratitude
- ☐ Encourage others
- ☐ Other (list below)

PRAYER

"Father, I know You care about my heart's desires. One of mine is . . .

AMEN."

REFLECTION

Define success with the Holy Spirit, not according to the world's standards—and you'll live a much happier, more satisfied life. What is your definition of success?

KINDNESS

Write about someone who made your life a little easier or better today.

SCRIPTURE

TAKE DELIGHT IN THE LORD,

AND HE WILL GIVE YOU

THE DESIRES OF YOUR HEART.

PSALM 37:4 NIV

GRATITUDE

Thank God for the experience in life that has drawn you closest to Him.

WELLNESS

Sip or guzzle? Every drop counts. How much water did you get today?

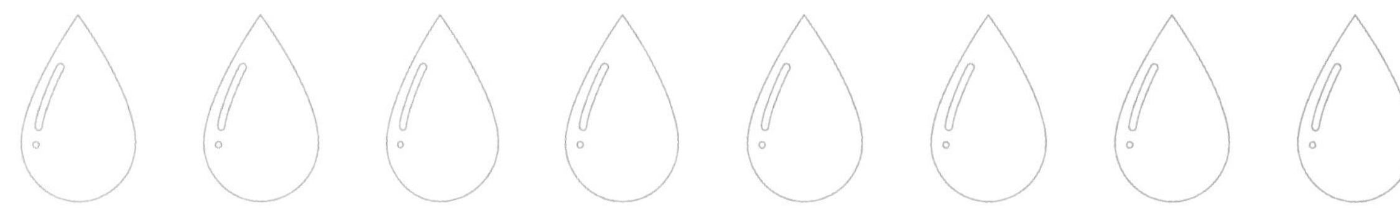

PRAYER

"Lord, I'm delighting in You in these ways today . . .

AMEN."

REFLECTION

God loves to delight those who delight in Him. What are some simple joys that you think God may have designed especially for you?

KINDNESS

Some of the best secrets are kept between you and God. Is there something encouraging you can do, say, or offer that no one else will know about? Write your ideas here, and then carry them out.

SCRIPTURE

FOR WE ARE HIS WORKMANSHIP,
CREATED IN CHRIST JESUS FOR GOOD WORKS,
WHICH GOD PREPARED BEFOREHAND
SO THAT WE WOULD WALK IN THEM.

EPHESIANS 2:10 NASB

GRATITUDE

Thank God for something you love about yourself.

WELLNESS

Fitness Goals

I am doing well with

I need to improve on

My strengths are

My weaknesses are

PRAYER

"God, regarding how You crafted me, my prayer is . . .

AMEN."

REFLECTION

Stay in tune. Be God's partner. Pay attention to the things that stir your heart in a special way. Then go out in joy and serve. What are some ways you think you've been designed to love others for Him?

KINDNESS

As you pray, does a friend or family member come to mind? God may be nudging you to reach out to them. Take a moment to text someone and remind them how important they are to you and God. Who did you text? What was their response?

SCRIPTURE

IF I FLEW ON MORNING'S WINGS
TO THE FAR WESTERN HORIZON,
YOU'D FIND ME IN A MINUTE–
YOU'RE ALREADY THERE WAITING!

PSALM 139:9-10 THE MESSAGE

GRATITUDE

Thank God for a special place you've been.

WELLNESS

How many hours did you sleep last night? ________ hours

PRAYER

"Lord, regarding how You're always with me, my prayer is . . .

AMEN."

REFLECTION

Leaving a hard situation without dealing with the root cause won't solve the problem. But trusting God always will. Have you surrendered a hard situation to Him before? How did it go?

KINDNESS

If you know God, then you know more about hope, love, and encouragement than most people! What kind words can you say to a stranger today? Write them down here and prepare for the moment to come.

SCRIPTURE

YOU GO BEFORE ME AND FOLLOW ME.
YOU PLACE YOUR HAND OF BLESSING ON MY HEAD.

PSALM 139:5 NLT

GRATITUDE

Thank God for the last person who gave you a hug.

WELLNESS

My stress management plan for the week is . . .

I can call (name a person who calms you)

I will (list activities you can do)

A positive statement I can say to myself is

PRAYER

"Lord, when I think of how You protect and guard me, my prayer is . . .

AMEN."

REFLECTION

God promises to be near. How does this affect your choices and the way you live life?

KINDNESS

When you pray, you are sharing your compassion with others and your heart with God. Offer to pray for someone who is worried or hurting today. Write about your experience.

SCRIPTURE

FOR YOU CREATED MY INMOST BEING;

YOU KNIT ME TOGETHER IN MY MOTHER'S WOMB.

PSALM 139:13 NIV

GRATITUDE

Thank God for the last baby you saw.

WELLNESS

How will you find rest today? (Check all that apply.)

- ☐ Take a nap. How long was the nap?
- ☐ Read a book. What was the title?
- ☐ Listen to music. Song or artist?
- ☐ Go to bed early. What time?
- ☐ Call a trusted friend. Who?
- ☐ Pray. What did you pray for?

PRAYER

"God, I know You made me with purpose. My prayer regarding my purpose is . . .

AMEN."

REFLECTION

God knew His plans for you when He knit you together. He had your whole life dreamed up. When was the last time you were giddy with anticipation? What was the situation?

KINDNESS

Find a way to make someone's day. Write your experience here.

SCRIPTURE

ASK, AND IT WILL BE GIVEN TO YOU;
SEEK, AND YOU WILL FIND; KNOCK,
AND IT WILL BE OPENED TO YOU.

MATTHEW 7:7 NASB

GRATITUDE

Thank God for the last thing you asked Him for.

WELLNESS

Soothing face wash, cucumber eye pads, or night cream? How have you "hugged" your skin today?

PRAYER

"Lord, here is my "ask, seek, knock" for today . . .

AMEN."

REFLECTION

We get discouraged if we pray for one ill person and that person doesn't get well. But what if we pray for one hundred ill people, and one of them is healed from a terminal illness? How do you feel about trust and perseverance in cases like that?

KINDNESS

Touch is one of the most vulnerable senses we have. Today, ask a trusted family member, coworker, or friend if they could use a hug. Then write about your experience here.

SCRIPTURE

I AM CERTAIN THAT GOD,
WHO BEGAN THE GOOD WORK WITHIN YOU,
WILL CONTINUE HIS WORK
UNTIL IT IS FINALLY FINISHED ON THE DAY
WHEN CHRIST JESUS RETURNS.

PHILIPPIANS 1:6 NLT

GRATITUDE

Thank God for the last time you messed up (and the fact that you'll do better next time).

WELLNESS

What can you do today to help you feel healthy and strong?

- ☐ Read the Bible
- ☐ Exercise
- ☐ Go for a walk
- ☐ Practice gratitude
- ☐ Drink more water
- ☐ Encourage others
- ☐ Other (list below)
- ☐ Other (list below)

PRAYER

"God, as you work on me from the inside out, my prayer is . . .

AMEN."

REFLECTION

Life isn't so much about getting there as it is about the journey! Where you are today is where God wants you. How content are you with the journey?

KINDNESS

Write about someone who made your life a little easier or better today.

SCRIPTURE

EVERYONE SHOULD BE
QUICK TO LISTEN,
SLOW TO SPEAK AND
SLOW TO BECOME ANGRY.

JAMES 1:19 NIV

GRATITUDE

Thank God for the last kind word you heard.

WELLNESS

Sip or guzzle? Every drop counts. How much water did you get today?

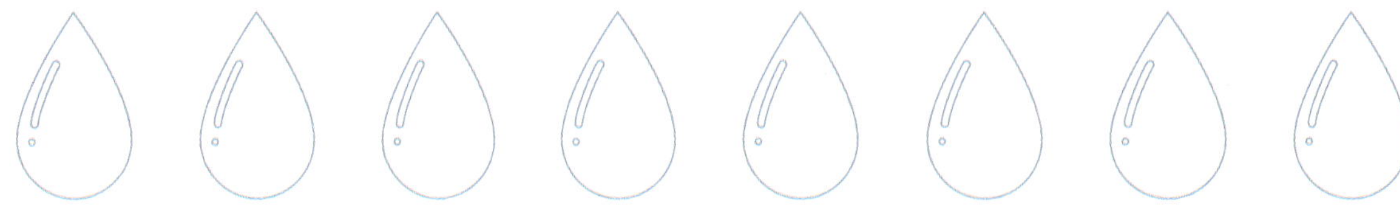

PRAYER

“Lord, as I grow in listening to others, my prayer is . . .

AMEN.”

REFLECTION

One of the best ways to be a good friend is to be the kind of friend you yourself would like to have. Are you happy in your friendships or wanting to grow? Why?

KINDNESS

Some of the best secrets are kept between you and God. Is there something encouraging you can do, say, or offer that no one else will know about? Write your ideas here, and then carry them out.

SCRIPTURE

BE STILL,

AND KNOW THAT I AM GOD.

PSALM 46:10 NIV

GRATITUDE

Thank God for your favorite place to relax.

WELLNESS

Fitness Goals

I am doing well with

I need to improve on

My strengths are

My weaknesses are

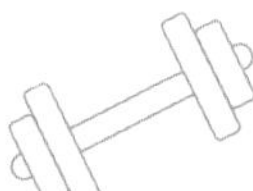

PRAYER

God, today I'm choosing to believe that You are the God of . . .

AMEN.

REFLECTION

To know is a verb, meaning it's something we do. What do you think it means to deliberately know that God is who He says He is?

KINDNESS

As you pray, does a friend or family member come to mind? God may be nudging you to reach out to them. Take a moment to text someone and remind them how important they are to you and God. Who did you text? What was their response?

SCRIPTURE

YOU WILL MAKE KNOWN TO ME THE WAY OF LIFE;
IN YOUR PRESENCE IS FULLNESS OF JOY;
IN YOUR RIGHT HAND THERE ARE PLEASURES FOREVER.

PSALM 16:11 NASB

GRATITUDE

Thank God for the last thing you laughed about.

WELLNESS

How many hours did you sleep last night? ______ hours

PRAYER

"Lord, when I think of living in the "fullness of joy," my prayer is . . .

AMEN."

REFLECTION

How have you experienced peace during a hard time?

KINDNESS

If you know God, then you know more about hope, love, and encouragement than most people! What kind words can you say to a stranger today? Write them down here and prepare for the moment to come.

SCRIPTURE

LOVE IS PATIENT AND KIND.

I CORINTHIANS 13:4 NLT

GRATITUDE

Thank God for the last person who was patient with you.

WELLNESS

My stress management plan for the week is . . .

I can call (name a person who calms you)

I will (list activities you can do)

A positive statement I can say to myself is

PRAYER

"Father, teach me patience and kindness . . .

AMEN."

REFLECTION

When in your life have you felt most loved?

KINDNESS

When you pray, you are sharing your compassion with others and your heart with God. Offer to pray for someone who is worried or hurting today. Write about your experience.

SCRIPTURE

IN REPENTANCE AND REST IS YOUR SALVATION,
IN QUIETNESS AND TRUST IS YOUR STRENGTH.

ISAIAH 30:15 NIV

GRATITUDE

Thank God for the last time you were forgiven.

WELLNESS

How will you find rest today? (Check all that apply.)

- ☐ Take a nap. How long was the nap?
- ☐ Read a book. What was the title?
- ☐ Listen to music. Song or artist?
- ☐ Go to bed early. What time?
- ☐ Call a trusted friend. Who?
- ☐ Pray. What did you pray for?

PRAYER

"Father, as I learn to rest and trust You, my prayer is . . .

AMEN."

REFLECTION

The mercy of God is there for the taking. He simply asks that you trust Him. Do you often think of repentance, rest, quietness, and trust as qualities He expects of you? Explain.

KINDNESS

Find a way to make someone's day. Write your experience here.

SCRIPTURE

WHETHER YOU EAT OR DRINK,

OR WHATEVER YOU DO,

DO ALL THINGS FOR THE GLORY OF GOD.

I CORINTHIANS 10:31 NASB

GRATITUDE

Thank God for the food on your table today.

WELLNESS

Soothing face wash, cucumber eye pads, or night cream? How have you "hugged" your skin today?

PRAYER

"Lord, regarding doing all things for Your glory, my prayer is . . .

AMEN."

REFLECTION

There's a lot we learn in the beginning that serves to get us started, but we make adjustments as we internalize and learn. How have you grown as you've discovered who God is?

KINDNESS

Touch is one of the most vulnerable senses we have. Today, ask a trusted family member, coworker, or friend if they could use a hug. Then write about your experience here.

SCRIPTURE

THE LORD HAS TOLD YOU WHAT IS GOOD,
AND THIS IS WHAT HE REQUIRES OF YOU:
TO DO WHAT IS RIGHT, TO LOVE MERCY,
AND TO WALK HUMBLY WITH YOUR GOD.

MICAH 6:8 NLT

GRATITUDE

Thank God for His boundaries and guidelines.

WELLNESS

What can you do today to help you feel healthy and strong?

- ☐ Read the Bible
- ☐ Go for a walk
- ☐ Drink more water
- ☐ Other (list below)
- ☐ Exercise
- ☐ Practice gratitude
- ☐ Encourage others
- ☐ Other (list below)

PRAYER

Father, as I consider justice, kindness, and humility, my prayer is . . .

AMEN.

REFLECTION

God's ways are always best. How can you enact justice, kindness, and humility in your day today?

KINDNESS

Write about someone who made your life a little easier or better today.

SCRIPTURE

GREAT IS OUR LORD AND MIGHTY IN POWER;

HIS UNDERSTANDING HAS NO LIMIT.

PSALM 147:5 NIV

GRATITUDE

Thank God for a decision you feel good about.

WELLNESS

Sip or guzzle? Every drop counts. How much water did you get today?

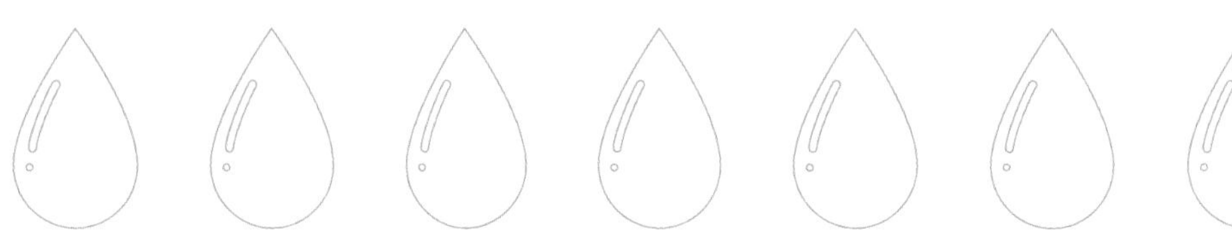

PRAYER

God, when I think about how much You see and understand, my prayer is . . .

AMEN.

REFLECTION

God does not fit into any size box we try to make for Him. You can dream big, but He can do bigger! Write the biggest dream for yourself that you can think of here. Then watch Him do more.

KINDNESS

Some of the best secrets are kept between you and God. Is there something encouraging you can do, say, or offer that no one else will know about? Write your ideas here, and then carry them out.

SCRIPTURE

WE LOVE, BECAUSE HE FIRST LOVED US.

I JOHN 4:19 NASB

GRATITUDE

Thank God for someone you know who is hard to love.

WELLNESS

Fitness Goals

I am doing well with

I need to improve on

My strengths are

My weaknesses are

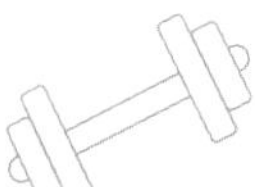

PRAYER

"Lord, when I think of how You loved me first, my prayer is . . .

AMEN."

REFLECTION

Are you hungry for more relationships? What are some ways you can reach out and connect with others? What are some ways you can share God's love?

KINDNESS

As you pray, does a friend or family member come to mind? God may be nudging you to reach out to them. Take a moment to text someone and remind them how important they are to you and God. Who did you text? What was their response?

SCRIPTURE

BY YOUR WORDS
I CAN SEE WHERE I'M GOING;
THEY THROW A BEAM OF LIGHT
ON MY DARK PATH.

PSALM 119:105 THE MESSAGE

GRATITUDE

Thank God for your eyes.

WELLNESS

How many hours did you sleep last night? ______ hours

PRAYER

Lord, as I read Your Word today, help me to see . . .

AMEN.

REFLECTION

Do you enjoy reading the Bible? What is one challenge you face when reading it? What benefits do you get from reading it?

KINDNESS

If you know God, then you know more about hope, love, and encouragement than most people! What kind words can you say to a stranger today? Write them down here and prepare for the moment to come.

SCRIPTURE

HE WILL ORDER HIS ANGELS

TO PROTECT YOU WHEREVER YOU GO.

PSALM 91:11 NLT

GRATITUDE

Thank God for the ways He protects you.

WELLNESS

My stress management plan for the week is . . .

I can call (name a person who calms you)

I will (list activities you can do)

A positive statement I can say to myself is

PRAYER

"God, as I step out in faith today, my prayer is . . .

AMEN."

REFLECTION

God cares so much for you and is constantly watching over you. Are you aware of His presence very often, or is that an area you want to grow in?

KINDNESS

When you pray, you are sharing your compassion with others and your heart with God. Offer to pray for someone who is worried or hurting today. Write about your experience.

SCRIPTURE

LET YOUR LIGHT SHINE BEFORE OTHERS,
THAT THEY MAY SEE YOUR GOOD DEEDS
AND GLORIFY YOUR FATHER IN HEAVEN.

MATTHEW 5:16 NIV

GRATITUDE

Thank God for the last person who was kind to you.

WELLNESS

How will you find rest today? (Check all that apply.)

- ☐ Take a nap. How long was the nap?
- ☐ Read a book. What was the title?
- ☐ Listen to music. Song or artist?
- ☐ Go to bed early. What time?
- ☐ Call a trusted friend. Who?
- ☐ Pray. What did you pray for?

PRAYER

"Lord, help me shine my light in these ways . . .

AMEN."

REFLECTION

Never be afraid to shine. But hide yourself in the Lord first. That way, you'll know that what shines through you is a true glimpse of heaven. Do you believe your light makes a difference?

KINDNESS

Find a way to make someone's day. Write your experience here.

SCRIPTURE

NOW TO HIM WHO IS ABLE
TO DO FAR MORE ABUNDANTLY BEYOND
ALL THAT WE ASK OR THINK,
ACCORDING TO THE POWER THAT WORKS WITHIN US,
TO HIM BE THE GLORY.

EPHESIANS 3:20-21 NASB

GRATITUDE

Thank God for the last time you were overwhelmed with happiness.

WELLNESS

Soothing face wash, cucumber eye pads, or night cream? How have you "hugged" your skin today?

PRAYER

God, when I think of Your power in me and what we can accomplish together, my prayer is . . .

AMEN.

REFLECTION

Whatever we dream, God can do bigger. If you knew you would succeed at your wildest hopes and plans, what would you set out to do today?

KINDNESS

Touch is one of the most vulnerable senses we have. Today, ask a trusted family member, coworker, or friend if they could use a hug. Then write about your experience here.

SCRIPTURE

BE STRONG IN THE LORD
AND IN HIS MIGHTY POWER.

EPHESIANS 6:10 NLT

GRATITUDE

Thank God for making you strong.

WELLNESS

What can you do today to help you feel healthy and strong?

- ☐ Read the Bible
- ☐ Go for a walk
- ☐ Drink more water
- ☐ Other (list below)
- ☐ Exercise
- ☐ Practice gratitude
- ☐ Encourage others
- ☐ Other (list below)

PRAYER

"Lord, regarding the strength I have in You, my prayer is . . .

AMEN."

REFLECTION

The Lord remains our shield and protector throughout our lives. We can be strong, because we're riding sidecar with our powerful Father! Do you value strength? What does being strong mean to you?

KINDNESS

Write about someone who made your life a little easier or better today.

SCRIPTURE

WHAT IS IMPOSSIBLE WITH MAN

IS POSSIBLE WITH GOD.

LUKE 18:27 NIV

GRATITUDE

Thank God for an impossible situation.

WELLNESS

Sip or guzzle? Every drop counts. How much water did you get today?

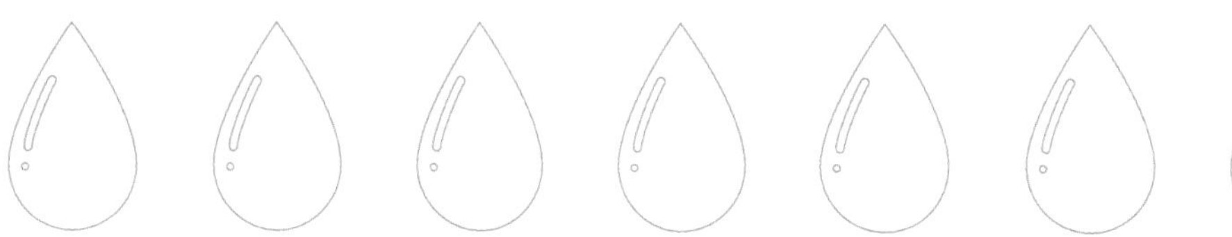

PRAYER

Lord, today I place this impossible situation in Your hands . . .

AMEN.

REFLECTION

If you spend any time considering what would be impossible without God, you'll be in awe again and again. What impossible things have you done lately?

KINDNESS

Some of the best secrets are kept between you and God. Is there something encouraging you can do, say, or offer that no one else will know about? Write your ideas here, and then carry them out.

SCRIPTURE

THESE THINGS I HAVE SPOKEN TO YOU
SO THAT MY JOY MAY BE IN YOU,
AND THAT YOUR JOY MAY BE MADE FULL.

JOHN 15:11 NASB

GRATITUDE

Thank God for wanting the very best for you.

WELLNESS

Fitness Goals

I am doing well with

I need to improve on

My strengths are

My weaknesses are

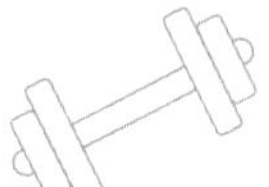

PRAYER

"Father, joy can be hard to find. Regarding my joy in You, my prayer is . . .

AMEN."

REFLECTION

God wants the very, very best for His children, including lasting joy! What makes you happiest? And when have you felt the deepest joy?

KINDNESS

As you pray, does a friend or family member come to mind? God may be nudging you to reach out to them. Take a moment to text someone and remind them how important they are to you and God. Who did you text? What was their response?

SCRIPTURE

THE LORD KEEPS WATCH
OVER YOU AS YOU COME AND GO,
BOTH NOW AND FOREVER.

PSALM 121:8 NLT

GRATITUDE

Thank God for your home.

WELLNESS

How many hours did you sleep last night? ________ hours

PRAYER

God, as I travel form one place to another, my prayer is . . .

AMEN.

REFLECTION

Even as you leave the safety of home, God will go with you. If you could travel anywhere, for any purpose, where would you go?

KINDNESS

If you know God, then you know more about hope, love, and encouragement than most people! What kind words can you say to a stranger today? Write them down here and prepare for the moment to come.

SCRIPTURE

DEAR FRIENDS,
LET US LOVE ONE ANOTHER,
FOR LOVE COMES FROM GOD.

I JOHN 4:7 NIV

GRATITUDE

Thank God for love.

WELLNESS

My stress management plan for the week is . . .

I can call (name a person who calms you)

I will (list activities you can do)

A positive statement I can say to myself is

PRAYER

"Lord, teach me to love people like You do . . .

AMEN."

REFLECTION

How does knowing that your love comes straight from the source, God, affect your desire and ability to love others?

KINDNESS

When you pray, you are sharing your compassion with others and your heart with God. Offer to pray for someone who is worried or hurting today. Write about your experience.

SCRIPTURE

REJOICE ALWAYS, PRAY WITHOUT CEASING,

IN EVERYTHING GIVE THANKS;

FOR THIS IS THE WILL OF GOD

FOR YOU IN CHRIST JESUS.

I THESSALONIANS 5:16-18 NASB

GRATITUDE

Thank God for the best and worst things that have happened this week.

WELLNESS

How will you find rest today? (Check all that apply.)

- ☐ Take a nap. How long was the nap?
- ☐ Read a book. What was the title?
- ☐ Listen to music. Song or artist?
- ☐ Go to bed early. What time?
- ☐ Call a trusted friend. Who?
- ☐ Pray. What did you pray for?

PRAYER

"Lord, regarding rejoicing, praying, and giving thanks, here's where I need the most help . . .

AMEN."

REFLECTION

Every experience we walk through with God has value and meaning to Him. Do you find it easy or hard to rejoice through every circumstance?

KINDNESS

Find a way to make someone's day. Write your experience here.

SCRIPTURE

THE LORD IS GOOD
TO THOSE WHO DEPEND ON HIM,
TO THOSE WHO SEARCH FOR HIM.

LAMENTATIONS 3:25 NLT

GRATITUDE

Thank God for His goodness toward you.

WELLNESS

Soothing face wash, cucumber eye pads, or night cream? How have you "hugged" your skin today?

PRAYER

"Lord, as I seek You, my prayer is . . .

AMEN."

REFLECTION

God isn't the kind of leader who says one thing and does another. How does knowing you can trust Him completely affect your willingness to accept a challenge or go on an adventure?

KINDNESS

Touch is one of the most vulnerable senses we have. Today, ask a trusted family member, coworker, or friend if they could use a hug. Then write about your experience here.

SCRIPTURE

THE LORD IS MY HELPER;

I WILL NOT BE AFRAID.

WHAT CAN MERE MORTALS DO TO ME?

HEBREWS 13:6 NIV

GRATITUDE

Thank God for the last time you were helped.

WELLNESS

What can you do today to help you feel healthy and strong?

- ☐ Read the Bible
- ☐ Go for a walk
- ☐ Drink more water
- ☐ Other (list below)
- ☐ Exercise
- ☐ Practice gratitude
- ☐ Encourage others
- ☐ Other (list below)

PRAYER

God, when others challenge me, I pray that . . .

AMEN.

REFLECTION

You have a special calling on your life—one designed by God, just for you. How has God gifted you to uniquely serve others?

KINDNESS

Write about someone who made your life a little easier or better today.

SCRIPTURE

YOU DO NOT HAVE
BECAUSE YOU DO NOT ASK.

JAMES 4:2 NASB

GRATITUDE

Thank God for something you want but don't have.

WELLNESS

Sip or guzzle? Every drop counts. How much water did you get today?

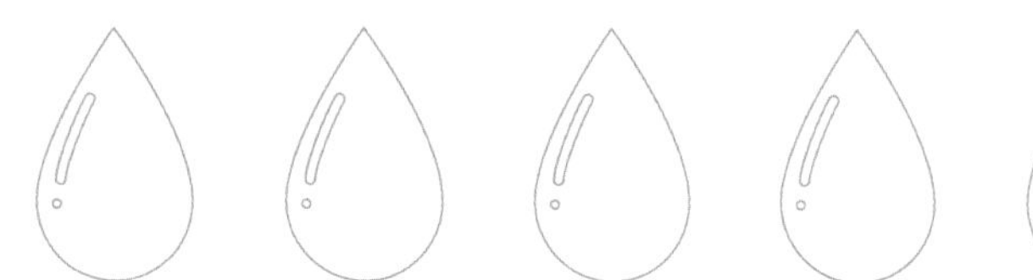

PRAYER

"God, today I ask . . .

AMEN."

REFLECTION

God's heart is for the gentle, meek, and mild. He waits for us to open our hands, with grateful hearts, and ask for what we desire. Is there anything specific you want to ask God for today?

KINDNESS

Some of the best secrets are kept between you and God. Is there something encouraging you can do, say, or offer that no one else will know about? Write your ideas here, and then carry them out.

SCRIPTURE

FOR THE WORD OF GOD
WILL NEVER FAIL.

LUKE 1:37 NLT

GRATITUDE

Thank God for your biggest dream.

WELLNESS

Fitness Goals

I am doing well with

I need to improve on

My strengths are

My weaknesses are

PRAYER

"Lord, please go to work on this situation . . .

AMEN."

REFLECTION

Impossible opportunities may be just the means by which God wants to show up and amaze you. What impossible things have you encountered lately?

KINDNESS

As you pray, does a friend or family member come to mind? God may be nudging you to reach out to them. Take a moment to text someone and remind them how important they are to you and God. Who did you text? What was their response?

SCRIPTURE

LET US THEN APPROACH
GOD'S THRONE OF GRACE WITH CONFIDENCE,
SO THAT WE MAY RECEIVE MERCY AND
FIND GRACE TO HELP US IN OUR TIME OF NEED.

HEBREWS 4:16 NIV

GRATITUDE

Thank God for the access He gives you through prayer.

WELLNESS

How many hours did you sleep last night? ________ hours

PRAYER

"Lord, today I'm drawing near to You . . .

AMEN."

REFLECTION

With God, we always have VIP access. All the way in—any time, any place, for any reason. No special badges or ID. If you know Jesus, you've got all the permission you need. How will this affect the way you pray to Him from now on?

KINDNESS

If you know God, then you know more about hope, love, and encouragement than most people! What kind words can you say to a stranger today? Write them down here and prepare for the moment to come.

SCRIPTURE

MAY THE GOD OF HOPE FILL YOU
WITH ALL JOY AND PEACE IN BELIEVING,
SO THAT YOU WILL ABOUND IN HOPE
BY THE POWER OF THE HOLY SPIRIT.

ROMANS 15:13 NASB

GRATITUDE

Thank God for the people who encourage you.

WELLNESS

My stress management plan for the week is . . .

I can call (name a person who calms you)

I will (list activities you can do)

A positive statement I can say to myself is

PRAYER

Father, I could use an infusion of hope in this area . . .

AMEN.

REFLECTION

Hope is God's specialty. He invented it. When things looked bleak, Jesus came along bearing all the possibility of freedom and eternal life. Who do you know that needs hope today?

KINDNESS

When you pray, you are sharing your compassion with others and your heart with God. Offer to pray for someone who is worried or hurting today. Write about your experience.

All Things Possible: Inspirational Interactive Journal

First Edition, March 2022

Published by:

21154 Highway 16 East
Siloam Springs, AR 72761
dayspring.com

Compiled by: Trieste Vaillancourt
Cover Design by: Jessica Wei

Printed in Vietnam
Prime: J7486
ISBN: 978-1-64870-426-0